st Boniface
and his world

st Boniface
and his world

A booklet to commemorate
the thirteen hundredth
anniversary of his birth
at Crediton in Devon

DAVID KEEP

Design and maps by Ann Butcher
Illustrations by Lorraine Calaora

EXETER
The Paternoster Press
1979

ISBN 0-85364-276-1

AUSTRALIA
Emu Book Agencies Ltd.,
63 Berry Street, Granville, N.S.W., 2142

SOUTH AFRICA
Oxford University Press,
P.O. Box 1141,
Cape Town

Keep, David
  St. Boniface and his world.
  1. Boniface, *Saint, Abp of Mainz*
  I. Title
  270.2'092'4   BX4700.B7

ISBN 0-85364-276-1

Typeset in 12 on 14 Paladium by Photoprint, Paignton, Devon,
and printed in Great Britain for The Paternoster Press Ltd.,
Paternoster House, 3, Mount Radford Crescent, Exeter, Devon.

contents

*An abbot's staff
from Fulda which
may have belonged
to St. Boniface*

introduction

for adults only

This booklet has been written to commemorate the birth of St. Boniface at Crediton in 680 AD. He became a monk, first at Exeter then at Nursling in Hampshire, before going abroad as a missionary and as an agent of the Pope in converting the heathen and uniting the church. Boniface built up a strong church in the Frankish Empire. At the age of seventy-four he was martyred in the north of the Netherlands. On the continent he has been respected as the apostle of Germany — of far more significance to the church in Europe than Augustine was in England. His name ranks with that of Newton as the greatest Englishman ever. In his own country he has been neglected. This was partly because most of his work was abroad, and partly because at the reformation he was portrayed as an agent of the Pope restricting the religious freedom of the Germans.

In our ecumenical age we may reassess the work of the Saint and see him as fighting for unity, order, morality and peace in the face of tribal warfare and often savage religious practices. People in Devon would like to see him adopted as the symbol of united Europe. Certainly he represents the struggle of Christianity against that paganism which is not so much new as natural.

The work which follows is intended for three groups. Chapter One is a simple outline of the life of the Saint which many children in junior schools will be able to read. Chapters Two and Three amplify this with an outline of the life of the time. This will be useful to more able middle school children and at the same time provides a summary for interested adults. The fourth chapter is for visitors to Devon. There is a brief booklist. The serious student will find further references in the works listed.

chapter 1

the life of st Boniface

The English Monk

The first story of the life of Boniface was written about ten years after his death. Later monks added new stories to Willibald's book. Some of these are legends, but they help us to understand how important the Saint was. One of these tells us that Boniface was born at Crediton in 680. He was baptised Winfrith, the friend of peace. The Saxons had just won Devon from the Britons and wanted to live in peace.

When Winfrith was five he asked his father if he could become a monk. This was the only way to learn to read and write. If you try to make a quill pen, you will find how hard it is! Kings like Alfred and Charlemagne found it very hard to learn to read. Winfrith's father was rich and wanted his son to be a merchant. He fell ill though, and changed his mind. He sent the boy to the new monastery at Exeter. Winfrith had chosen a life of study and prayer rather than trade and fighting.

By the time he was twenty, Winfrith had read the books at Exeter. It took a long time to build up a library when all the books were written carefully by hand. Abbot Wulfhard sent him to the big monastery at Nursling near the important city of Winchester. The young monk walked along the same roads as we use today. He may have stayed the night with the priests at Ilminster and Salisbury. There were many more forests and fewer villages then. It was a hard journey and Winfrith never saw Devon again.

There is only a tiny church at Nursling now and it is difficult to-imagine the busy monastery. The monks had services six times each day. They had to learn their lessons by heart and make new copies of books. Winfrith was a favourite teacher. He wrote a new book to help boys learn Latin and told stories to help explain the Bible. When he was thirty he became a 'preacher', or priest.

In those days monks and priests worked for the king as well as for the church. They had to do all the writing and look after the important papers. Abbot Winbert was an adviser at the court of King Ine. Monks also acted as royal messengers. Soon after Winfrith became a priest there was a civil war in Wessex. Ine wanted help from the Archbishop of Canterbury. He sent Winfrith to explain the problem. The young monk did this so well that he was made a member of the royal council. When Winbert died in 718, all the monks wanted him to be the new Abbot, but he already had other plans.

The Missionary

News travelled slowly in those days and people had more time to think about it. The Anglo-Saxons had only been Christians for just over a hundred years. People still told tales of the old gods who became the ghosts and fairies of the marshes and forests. The Saxons in Germany and the Frisians in Holland were still pagans. The monks at Nursling heard about the Northumbrian monk Willibrord who had gone to preach near Utrecht in 692. Winfrith felt that God was calling him to become a missionary as well.

In 716 he set out on his first journey. Two friends went with him. One of them was a short man called Lull. They went north to London where they knew they would find a ship. London was not a big town then, but there were still parts of the Roman walls and some stone houses. Their ship took them across the North Sea and up the river Rhine. From their landing place they walked to Utrecht, the capital of Radbod, the king of the Frisians.

Radbod was not pleased to see them. He was at war with Charles Martel, the ruler of the Franks. He had once nearly become a Christian, but when the priest told him his father was in hell, he said he would join his family. Now he was destroying the churches the Franks had built and making the old sacrifices. He listened to the monks from Wessex, but would not change his plans. Winfrith toured the country in the summer and autumn and then returned to Nursling. He decided he would try again one day.

In 718 Winfrith set out again. This time he went to Rome to visit the Pope. He never returned to England. He had to ask permission from the new abbot, Stephen, and Daniel the Bishop of Winchester. The bishop gave him a letter to take to the Pope. This had a secret sign on it so that the Pope would know that Winfrith was really a friend of the

bishop. The small party of monks went to London again, but this time landed on the river Canche near Le Touquet. They had a long way to walk across Europe, but they were well cared for in the great halls of bishops, lords and monasteries. We know that Winfrith did not drink beer or wine. The wells and streams were cleaner then than in the later middle ages. The Franks looked after their English guests well. The Lombards of north Italy were more dangerous, but the monks crossed the Alps and reached Rome safely early in 719.

Rome was the most important place for pilgrims in Europe. Chris-

St. Boniface baptising converts: based on an eleventh century Fulda sacrament book

tians went to see where St. Peter and St. Paul had died. The bishops wanted to make it the centre of the church. It was hard to keep contact with each other in times of war. The Pope Gregory II asked Winfrith to find out what was happening to the churches in the parts of Germany not ruled by the Franks. Winfrith agreed. The Pope gave him a new name, Boniface, which means 'speaker of good'. Boniface set off again across Lombardy to Bavaria and Thuringia. Irish monks had been there and left churches, but there was no bishop. Some kept the old date for Easter as the English had before the Synod of Whitby in 664. Some mixed Christian with pagan worship. Many priests had wives. Boniface told them how to run their churches properly.

Boniface was working for the Pope. He was also keen to spread the gospel in all of Europe. He went west to visit France. When he heard that Radbod was dead he remembered his vow in Frisia and went north to find Willibrord. For three years the two English missionaries worked together. They destroyed pagan shrines and built churches.

Sometimes they turned temples into Christian churches. In other places they built simple wooden halls. Willibrord was over sixty years old. He wanted Boniface to become bishop in his place. Boniface remembered that he was working for the Pope. He thought he was not old enough to be a bishop. Sadly, Willibrord let him go.

Boniface was still not satisfied. He went back to the Saxon tribes to a town called Amoeneburg in Hesse. There he converted the princes, who were twins called Dettic and Devrulf. The people became Christian and Boniface built a church. He wrote a long letter to the Pope. The Pope sent the messenger back with orders for Boniface to return to Rome.

Boniface made the long journey to Rome for the second time. He walked through the lands of the Franks, then Burgundy, north Italy and the lands ruled by the emperor of Constantinople. These were dangerous because the soldiers there sometimes stole if their pay was late. Pope Gregory was pleased to see Boniface. He asked him about his beliefs. Boniface wrote them down and read them to the Pope. Gregory was very pleased and asked Boniface how to preach to pagans. The Englishman answered so well that Gregory decided to make him bishop for all the German lands. Boniface was made bishop on St. Andrew's day in the year 722 or 723. The Pope wrote to Charles Martel asking him to help the new bishop.

Boniface went back north with the support of the most important Christian leader and the strongest king in Europe. He had to deal with free counts and kings in Germany, and he did not have a cathedral or headquarters. He travelled round the churches of Hesse and laid hands in confirmation on those he found to be good Christians. Others of them went on worshipping the old gods and making sacrifices. Boniface decided to challenge them. He heard about a great tree at Geismar which was called 'Thor's oak'. It may have been struck by lightening. Boniface found people worshipping the tree, seized an axe and started to cut it down. Willibald wrote that as soon as he had made a vee-shaped cut, a great wind dashed the old trunk to the ground and it split into the shape of a cross. A later German legend tells that a tiny fir sprang up among the roots. This was the first Christmas tree. Boniface used the oak to build St. Peter's Chapel.

When the people saw that Thor did no harm to Boniface they lost their faith in the old gods. Hesse had become Christian, so Boniface

went south to Thuringia. The duke had died there, and the counts were fighting. Boniface managed to bring them to a council. They agreed to keep the peace and punish those who broke the laws or taught false religion. Boniface went round Thuringia preaching and building churches. He started his first monastery at Ohrdruf. Boniface worked very hard and was often tired and hungry. News of his work reached England and many good men like Wigbert and Burghard came to help him. By 731 when Pope Gregory died, thousands of Thuringians had been baptised. Boniface sent some monks with letters to the new Pope. The following year Pope Gregory III sent the monks back. They brought letters and relics of saints to put in the new churches. They also brought a very special gift for Boniface. This was a pallium, a special white scarf with six crosses on it. These scarves were worn only by the Pope and his archbishops. Boniface was now an archbishop for all Germany and had to divide the country up and make bishops.

The Archbishop

Archbishop Boniface's first action was to build two large churches and monasteries. These were St. Peter's at Fritzlar and St. Michael's at Amoeneburg. He then went further south to visit Duke Hugobert of Bavaria. There he converted the followers of a false teacher called Eremwulf. Boniface was now fifty-eight and finding travel harder, but he set out to visit Rome for the third time. Gregory make him very welcome. People flocked to hear him preach so he stayed nearly a year. On his return journey in 739 he was a guest of King Liudprand of Lombardy and Odilo the new Duke of Bavaria.

Boniface was now the official agent, or Legate, of the Pope. He found the Bavarian churches in a mess. Some had made their own bishops and they taught different things. Boniface and Odilo called a synod and divided Bavaria into four districts. The Pope had already sent a bishop called Vivilo to Passau. Boniface made bishops for Salzburg, Regensburg and Freising. He then went on to the Saxons and made bishops for Buraburg in Hesse and Wurzburg and Erfurt in Thuringia. In two years he had organised the Catholic church in three of the German states.

In 741 the great Charles Martel died. His sons divided his lands. Carloman ruled the eastern, or German part. In 742 Boniface went to visit him and they held a synod for the church. They made rules that the people must marry properly in church, and that priests must not have wives. The next year Boniface held a synod at Estinnes and then went on to visit Carloman's brother Pepin. They held a synod for the churches in the French part of Frankland at Soissons, near Paris, in 744. The synod wanted to have three archbishops, but local rivalry cut this to one, Grimo of Rouen. Boniface expected to live in the important city of Cologne. The bishop of Mainz was sacked for killing a man and Boniface was sent there instead. Mainz was the chief cathedral of the eastern Franks until 785.

Boniface was helping to unite the Christians in Europe. The Arabs had attacked France from Spain. Charles Martel had beaten them at

The Cathedral of Fulda: the present church is in the baroque style of the eighteenth century

St. Boniface felling
Thor's oak

Tours in 732. This proved to be one of the most important battles in Europe, but Europe feared the Arabs and Turks for a thousand years. The peoples of Europe were made up of small tribes and did not like joining together. There are groups in all countries today trying to split from the central government. The Franks had been used to making their own bishops. Two of these were so difficult that Boniface sent their case to Rome. Their names were Aldebert and Clement.

A special synod met in Rome on 25th October 745. Boniface was too busy to go. He sent the priest Denehard with a letter and some books by Aldebert. There were two big problems. The first was that both men said they did not need to obey Boniface or the Pope. The second was that their teaching was not right. Just as we cannot drive on the wrong side of the road, so Boniface saw that the church must make rules for the wild world of warring tribes. Boniface and the Pope were trying to do for Europe what Moses had done for the Hebrews when he gave them the Ten Commandments.

The two false bishops were quite different. Aldebert, like Mohamet and Joseph Smith the Mormon, had had a vision of an angel. He claimed to be as good as the apostles and to be able to forgive sins. He built churches to his own name and had many followers. He said prayers to angels, most of whom the Pope said were demons. The Scot, Clement, taught only the Bible and took no notice of the books of the fathers of the church. He called himself a bishop and said all priests should marry. He taught that Jesus had saved all the sinners in hell. The Pope agreed with Boniface and said the two were no longer priests. He asked Pepin to keep them in prison out of the way. Boniface had united the churches of the Franks.

In 747 Boniface held his last synod. His friend Carloman was tired of being a ruler and went to Rome to become a monk. This left Pepin all the lands of the Franks, but he was not a king. In 739 his father had helped the Pope to fight the Lombards. In 751 the Pope asked for an army again. Pepin agreed if he could be King of the Franks. He sent Childeric II and his son, the last of the Merovingian kings into a monastery. Boniface anointed Pepin king as the prophet Samuel had anointed Saul and David. This ceremony, the chrism, is still used in our coronation service. In return Pepin gave the Abbey of Fulda to the Pope for ever. This was Boniface's favourite and he treated it as his home.

The Pope needed help as the emperor had called his soldiers back to

Constantinople. In 754 Pope Stephen rode to France himself to ask for help. He was met by the boy who was to become the first Holy Roman Emperor. The Pope anointed Pepin and his wife and sons again. In return the king signed a parchment giving the whole of Italy to the Pope. Until 1870 the popes were to be rulers of a large part of Italy as well as head of the church.

Boniface was not present at this great event. He was old and tired. We do not know whether he was at his cathedral at Mainz or watching over the building work at Fulda. Although he was seventy-four years

old and had built a strong church in France and Germany he still wanted to go back to the pagan Frisians. He knew his work was safe. Lull the Little was made archbishop and English friends were bishops of Eichstätt and Würzburg. Willibald of Eichstätt was a relative of the King of Kent and a cousin by marriage of Boniface. He has left us the story of a journey to see Jerusalem. He was not the author of the life of Boniface. The work of Boniface and his friends survives in the strong Christian churches of Europe today.

The martyrdom of St. Boniface: based on an eleventh century Fulda sacrament book

The Martyr

In 754 Boniface set out on his last journey. As on his first he went as a simple preacher of the gospel. We may still read his careful instructions to Lull about the building works in Thuringia and about his packing. Lull wept when he was told to put a shroud in with the books. The small party took a boat down the Rhine and across the

St. Boniface: based on a 1954 Netherlands stamp commemorating the 1200th anniversary of Boniface's martyrdom

Zuyder Zee. With Bishop Eoban of Utrecht he spent two summers destroying idols and baptising converts. On 4th June 755 he pitched camp near Dokkum in the far north of Friesland. He was going to confirm the local people. Instead of these, armed men attacked the camp at dawn on 5th June. You will have seen similar Red Indian raids in films on television. In the confusion, some of the servants wanted to fight. Boniface called to them to pray instead and to trust God. Later stories tell us that Boniface protected his head with a copy of the gospels. There is a collection of Christian writings with a sword-cut through the first page at Fulda.

The Frisians killed all the Christians they could. We do not know whether they were just robbers after the supplies in the ship, or pagans trying to stop the church from spreading. They got drunk on the wine in the boats and then fought over the booty. When they found the chests contained books and not treasure, they were angry and threw them into the marshes. Some of them were rescued later. The Christians in the rest of Frisia were so angry at the death of Boniface that they killed all the murderers and destroyed the pagan shrines all through their country.

The bodies of the martyrs were taken to Utrecht by boat. Lull had sent monks to fetch Boniface's body to Fulda. The count wanted to keep it in his cathedral, but changed his mind when the bell began to toll by itself. The monks rowed the corpse slowly to Mainz where a great crowd met it. They carried it to Fulda where it was buried in a new stone tomb. Willibald wrote that many sick people were healed at the tomb of the saint. He ended his book with the story of building a mound at Dokkum with a church on it dedicated to St. Paul and St. Boniface. He wrote that a clear spring rose on the spot where the saint had died.

Boniface had been a great missionary and bishop to the churches in Germany. Now he had become a martyr and a saint. Churches were called after him and pilgrims flocked to his tomb at Fulda, as they still do. Each time the church was made bigger, relics were sent to other churches. He is honoured in Italy, France, Germany and the Netherlands. No Englishman has done more in Europe. In an age when many Christian lands had been conquered by Moslem soldiers, Boniface had helped to build a united Christian Europe.

In England he has not been so well remembered. The Archbishop of Canterbury wrote to Lull promising to say special prayers on 5th June, but so far as we know, no English churches were dedicated to him until later. In the sixteenth century he was unpopular as a friend of the Pope. In the last hundred years many Catholics have come to England and at least twenty churches have been called after St. Boniface. These include their cathedral at Plymouth and their Parish church at Crediton. Now that Christians have come closer together, we may see Boniface as a great preacher and leader like St. Paul himself. He gave himself to the service of God and tried to follow Jesus's prayer that his followers should be one. Some people hope that Boniface will become a symbol for a united states of Europe.

chapter 2

the world of st Boniface

The Dark Ages

In 455 the city of Rome was destroyed by a tribe called the Vandals. This event gave a new word to Europe. In 476 the last emperor lost his throne and the Roman Empire survived only around Constantinople and in Asia and Africa. Europe was invaded by groups of tribes. These migrations were caused by the building of the Great Wall of China in 215 BC. The period from the fall of Rome to the end of the great Viking conquests in Russia, Normandy and Sicily is known as the 'Dark Ages'. We should remember that they are dark to us rather than the people at the time. We do not know very much about the period because only monks had the skill and time to write and many of their libraries were burned by the Norsemen. This was the age of heroes like King Arthur and his knights and Charlemagne and Roland. In the middle ages poets wrote books called *romances* about them. Historians today have to act like detectives and build up a picture from clues.

The easiest of these are, chronicles. We know a lot about Anglo-Saxon Christianity from Bede's famous 'Church History of the English People' which he finished at Jarrow in 731. Monks in Wessex kept up 'The Anglo-Saxon Chronicle' until 1154. There are 'Lives' of all the saints and great men, though these sometimes add miracles and legends to make their heroes seem more important. Norman historians like William of Malmesbury and Bishop Grandisson of Exeter added to the old lives, though they too made up stories to please pilgrims. The monks of Glastonbury used to claim that Jesus had been there as a boy, and all holy places attracted legends.

The second group of clues may be seen by everybody, but not always understood. These are the names given to towns and villages, and even to fields and lanes. In this way, we can still see the close connection between Cornwall and Brittany. Place names show us how little impact the Saxons had in Cornwall, and also where they used to worship their old gods. In Dorset there is a village called Winfrith Newburgh. We may guess that the family of Boniface had been there on their move westwards and his parents passed the name on to their son.

The third kind of clue may also be seen, though less easily. All around and under us there are mounds, roads and ditches which mark ancient boundaries. There are battlefields and graves. Some of these can be read by archaeologists, but they cannot easily be dated. Important new discoveries are still being made, like the Water Newton church treasure near Peterborough and one new fact can change a great deal of history. The childhood of Boniface in Devon is itself an important clue.

England in 700 AD

The Saxons first came to England in 449 AD. The chronicler wrote that 'Hengist and Horsa, invited by Vortigern, king of the Britons, came to Britain at the place which is called Ebbsfleet, first to the help of the Britons, but afterwards fought against them.'

They drove the Britons west and cut new farms in the forests. They set up kingdoms of Saxons and Angles, many of which survive in the names of our counties. Seven of these survived in the time of Boniface with Northumbria. Mercia and Kent were the most important. Northumbria was the cultural centre. Missionaries had converted most of the English from there. St. Wilfrid had united the churches to the Roman church calendar at the Synod of Whitby in 664 and had preached in Frisia in 678 on his way to Rome. The northern monasteries had the finest scholars, like Bede, and artists who produced the famous Lindisfarne gospels. Northumbria had improved the old Roman art preserved in Ireland and supplied all Europe until it fell to the Vikings.

Mercia was the strongest. Penda, who made the first pennies, had killed two kings of Northumbria before his death in 655. Offa was king 757 - 796. The great Charlemagne treated him as an equal. He built the famous wall along the Welsh border and ruled London. Mercian power helped to drive the Saxons further west.

Kent had the closest ties with the Franks, and the people there were a different tribe. Bede said they came from Jutland. Augustine began his mission there in 597 and Canterbury remains the centre of the

York

Jarrow
Wearmouth

NORTH UMBRRIA

ROMAN WALL

CUMBRIA
(BRITONS)

STRATHCLYDE
BRITONS
(NORTHERN WELSH)

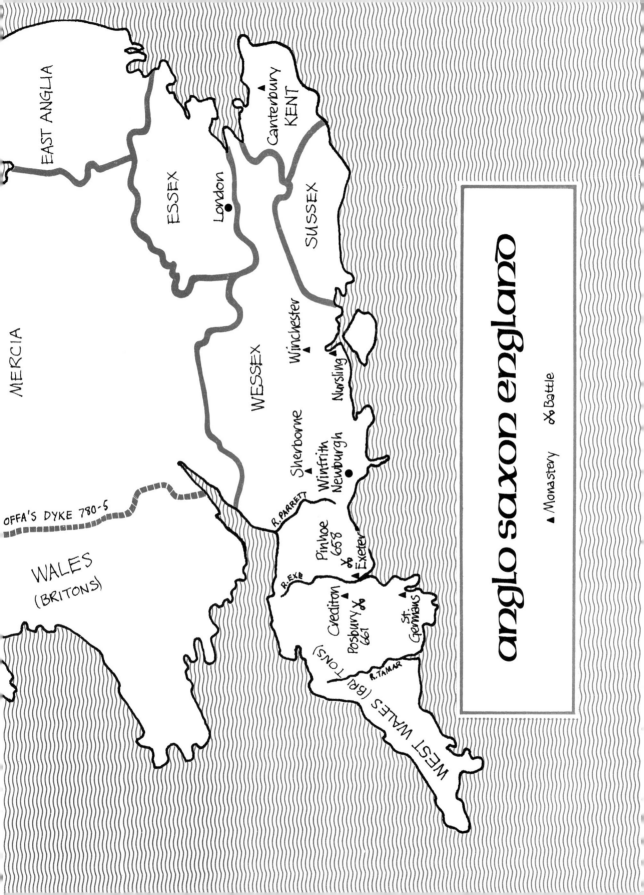

anglo saxon england

▲ Monastery   ⚔ Battle

EAST ANGLIA

MERCIA

ESSEX

London

WALES
(BRITONS)

OFFA'S DYKE 780-5

Canterbury
KENT

SUSSEX

WESSEX

Winchester ▲

Nursling ▲

Sherborne ▲

Winfrith
Newburgh ●

R. PARRETT

Pinhoe
658 ⚔

Exeter ▲

R. EXE

Crediton ▲

Posbury ⚔
661

St.
Germans ▲

R. TAMAR

WEST WALES (BRITONS)

Church of England.

Wessex was fighting for land in the west. Willibald's 'Life of St. Boniface' is the earliest evidence for the Saxons in Devon. He wrote that the boy was sent to the monastery at 'Adescancastra'. This is the Latin 'Isca castra' from which Exeter has come. John Grandisson, who was bishop 1327-69, had a new 'Legend of St. Boniface' written which added that he was born into a noble family at Kirton, or Crediton. We cannot prove this, but there are no other serious claims. The Saxons had not been in Devon very long. The chronicler wrote in 658: 'In this year Cenwealh fought against the Britons at Peonnan, and put them to flight to the Parret'.

The river runs north to Bridgwater, but we do not know where the battle was fought. For a long time it was accepted as Penselwood, but Professor W. G. Hoskins has suggested Pinhoe. In this case, the battle at 'Posentesbyrig' in 661 would be Posbury. This would have given them control of the Exe Valley, and the battle in 682 would have completed the conquest of Devon. Winfrith's parents would have been among the first settlers, which makes the name 'friend of peace', especially significant.

The monastery at Exeter could not have been very old when the boy Winfrith was sent to it. It was probably where the cathedral is now in the south-east corner of the Roman walls. According to William of Malmesbury, the Britons and Saxons lived side-by-side in Exeter until the tenth century. St. Petroc's was the British church, St. Sidwell's the Saxon. As a young monk Winfrith would have seen the problems of the different dates for Easter and the different forms of service. The bishop did not move to Exeter until 1050 when the old walls offered greater protection from the Danes, even though they had burned the monastery in 1003.

A monastery was founded at Crediton in 739 by King Ethelheard. Boniface's friend Daniel of Winchester signed the charter, so this may have been because of his birth there. When the diocese of Sherborne was divided in 909, bishops were made for Cornwall at St. Germans and Devon at Crediton. Cornwall was reunited with Devon from 1040 to 1877. For a hundred and forty years Crediton was the most important Christian centre west of Salisbury. This is the strongest evidence for the birth of the saint there. The parish church at Crediton, like de Grandisson's lovely church at Ottery St. Mary, still operates under a Royal Charter. This is one of the few hints of the importance of the monastic foundation there.

Europe in 700 AD

The Ural mountains in Russia are the eastern frontier of Europe. From them to the North Sea there is a great plain broken up by rivers. Across these rivers the peoples of Europe have fought and united. The history of modern Europe has been the story of the rivalry between Germany and France. When we look at the map of Europe in the time of Boniface, we see that the whole plain was the land of the Franks. This was divided into Neustria and Austrasia.

The Frankish kingdom was ruled by strong chieftains who farmed the land round their own halls, and like the Saxon kings, had their court where they were. Sometimes Neustria and Austrasia were divided, sometimes together. Both moved south towards the Burgundians and the Bavarians, and towards the Frisians to the north and the savage Saxons to the East. Modern France did not begin until after the Viking invasions of Normandy and the Hundred Years' War with the Anglo-Norman empire. The 'French' in 700 were a German tribe which had crossed the Rhine and taken over a little of the Roman culture. They had also become Christians. Their 'German' cousins to the north and east had not, and nor had the wild Slavs, who were so called as they were treated as slaves. Further south there were the east and west Goths who had conquered Rome and then set up their own Christian kingdoms. The Visigoths in Spain were defeated by the Moslem Moors. In Italy the Lombards set up a strong kingdom in the northern plain.

In theory in 700 the centre of Italy was still part of the eastern Roman empire ruled by the Exarch of Ravenna. So long as Constantinople had a strong fleet, the emperor kept control of the coast of the Adriatic. Pope Zacharias (741 - 752) was the last to speak Greek as his first language. After him, the popes looked to the king of the Franks for support and began to claim to be chief ruler of Italy. The pressure of the Moslems in Asia Minor and Spain moved the centre of power in Europe towards the north-west.

North of Italy and east of the Rhine there were the Bavarians, Thuringians, Hessians, Saxons and Frisians. They became more or less subjects of the Franks. Charlemagne completed their conversion with the sword. More than in England, their kingdoms survived; Bavaria until as late as 1918. Celtic monks, like St. Gall of north Switzerland,

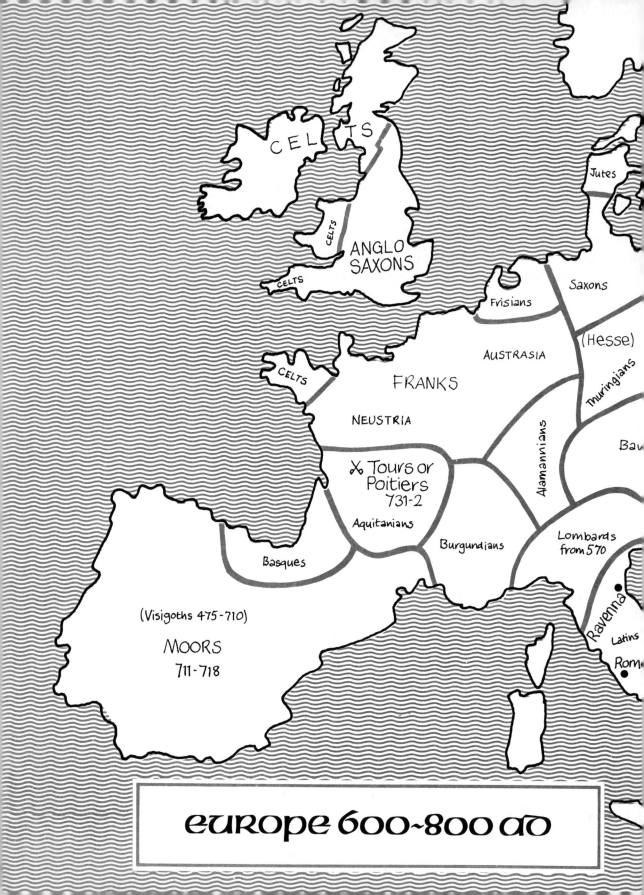

CELTS

Jutes

ANGLO
SAXONS

CELTS

CELTS

CELTS

Frisians

Saxons

(Hesse)

Thuringians

AUSTRASIA

FRANKS

NEUSTRIA

Alamannians

Bav

⚔ Tours or
Poitiers
731-2

Aquitanians

Burgundians

Lombards
from 570

Basques

Ravenna

(Visigoths 475-710)

Latins

MOORS
711-718

Rom

europe 600~800 ad

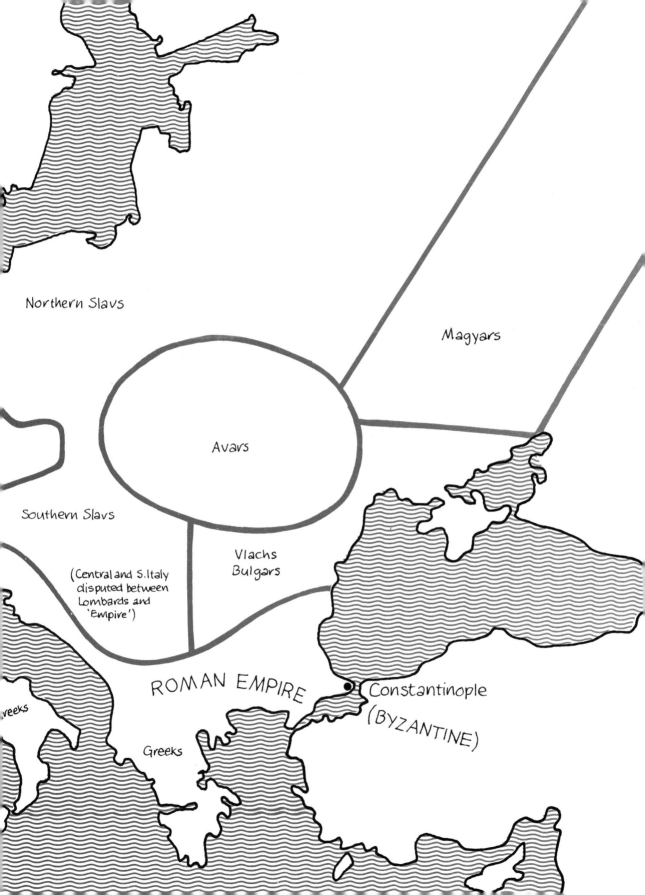

Northern Slavs

Magyars

Avars

Southern Slavs

Vlachs
Bulgars

(Central and S. Italy
disputed between
Lombards and
'Empire')

ROMAN EMPIRE

Constantinople
(BYZANTINE)

Greeks

Greeks

had preached with some success. Sometimes they practised two forms of religion together. The Franks too had been converted by Celts, either from Britain or from the lands they had conquered.

Europe after the fall of Rome was like a kaleidoscope. Every few years it was shaken, and a different coloured map appeared. Many places stayed the same when their rulers changed. On the map, the Celts were driven to Ireland, Cornwall and Brittany but they must have continued in France under Frankish rule. Much of the fighting was between people of the same tribe to gain power. The farm-

The Roman triple goddesses from the fort at Housesteads, Northumberland

workers, often slaves, would have done and believed what they were told, and kept their old traditions to themselves. When I look at the statue of the Trinity in Caen I am reminded of the triple Roman goddesses at Housesteads on the Roman wall and the Celtic triple goddess. The Christian monks preached in a fertile soil and tied Europe together with a crude form of the Latin language. The history of Europe is a story of migration and the blending of races.

The Old Religion

Most of what we know about the old religions of Europe comes from books by Christian writers who opposed them. Only in Iceland were the stories of the Norse gods told long enough for them to be written down, and by then they had an unhappy ending. This was the story of 'the twilight of the gods' involving their death. We cannot be sure that the Saxons had the same stories as the Norsemen, but scholars have found similar beliefs in all old religions at least as far as India. Roman writers tried to find the same sort of gods in Greek and German religion. We may see this if we compare the names of the days of the week in French and English. Religion was connected with the weather and with fertility and harvest. Men had no control over these mysteries. They feared the power of the sea and of rivers. Human sacrifices were made when bridges were built after the Moslem conquest of Bosnia in the fifteenth century. The story of the three billygoats Gruff is a reminder of the ancient fear of river-crossings and their gods, as are the churches on old bridges like St. Edmund's in Exeter. The martyrdom of St. Sidwell of Exeter and St. Hieritha of Chittlehampton with sickles may reflect the same fertilisation of the fields with blood as do the corn-dollies which we hang in our homes without thinking about them. The ending of human and animal sacrifice was one of the great achievements of Christianity.

The days of the week are a useful guide to Saxon religion. The worship of the Sun and the Moon was common to all religions. It is easy to find Christian hymns which call Jesus the sun, or the light of the world. We are not sure how the Saxons worshipped them. The gods certainly changed their roles in the order of things. Tuesday is called after Tiw, or Tiwaz. He was the great sky-father. In India he was called Dyaus, in Greece Zeus and in Latin his name became 'deus', a god. The Romans worshipped him as Jove. There is more difference in the spelling than in the sound of the names for the great god. He is found in place-names like Tysoe in Warwickshire. Later Woden became the chief god and Tiw became the god of war. This is why the Germans named the Roman Mar's-day (mardi) Tuesday.

The god Woden seems to have been the most widely worshipped by the Saxons and most of their kings claimed to be descended from him. He may have begun as the wind and storm god who led his wild hunt across the sky. In the north he was called Odin, and he was linked with the Roman god Mercury (mercredi is French for Wednesday). The norse stories say that he was hanged in order to gain the secret of writing in runes and healing with herbs. He was supposed to talk to

Synod
of Whitby
664

London

Born 680
Crediton
Exeter
Nursling
Canterbury

Cuentewick
718

Soissons
(Council 744)

⚔ Battle of Tours
(or Poitiers)
731-732

the Journeys of
st Boniface

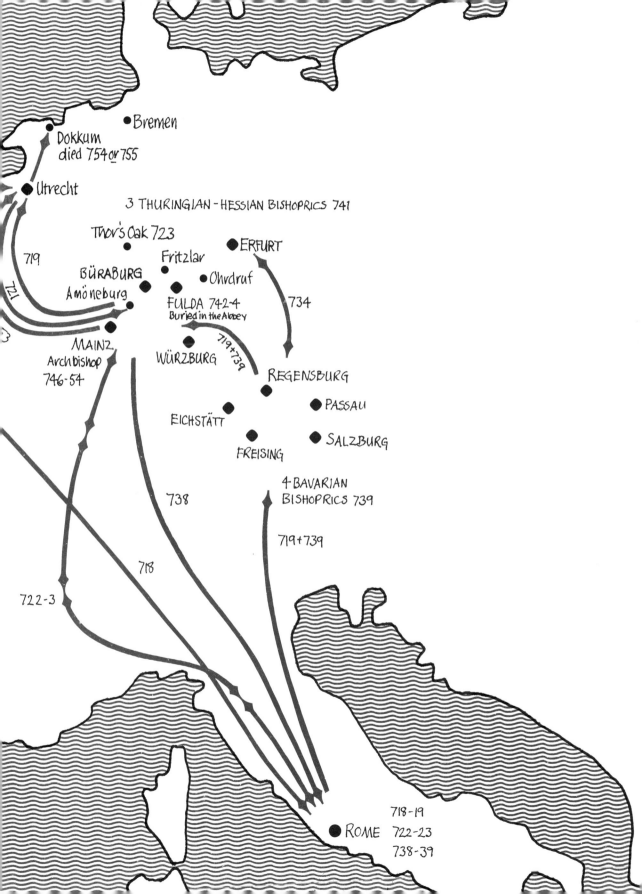

• Bremen

Dokkum
died 754 or 755

Utrecht

3 THURINGIAN – HESSIAN BISHOPRICS 741

719

721

Thor's Oak 723
Fritzlar   ● ERFURT
BÜRABURG   ● Ohrdruf
Amöneburg

FULDA 742-4
Buried in the Abbey   734

719 + 739

MAINZ
Archbishop   WÜRZBURG   REGENSBURG
746-54
● PASSAU

EICHSTÄTT   ● SALZBURG

FREISING

4 BAVARIAN
BISHOPRICS 739

738

719 + 739

718

722-3

ROME   718-19
        722-23
        738-39

hanged men, some of whom like the famous Tollund man in Denmark may have been sacrifices. Some of the places called after gallows, like Heavitree in Exeter, may have been places of sacrifice as well as of punishment. The skill of his priests became the spells and magic of the middle ages and the tales of the wild hunt of the Valkyries became the ghost stories of headless huntsmen and phantom coaches in later centuries.

English place-names suggest that the god Thunor, or Thor the thunderer, was the most popular god of the east, south and west Saxons. Like the Hindu weather god Indra, he was said to have red hair. His name was given to Jove's day in the Roman calendar (jeudi). Because he could smash great trees he was said to have a magic hammer which returned to his hand. Children and animals today feel the same fear of lightning as men did in the past. The Saxons said Thor was the child of Woden and Jorth, the earth. This was the god Boniface challenged at Geismar. The people expected him to be struck by a thunderbolt. John Bunyan still believed that God killed wicked people like that, and the oath 'strike me dead' survived for a long time. It may be that England adopted St. George because of the stories of Thor. One of his tasks was to kill the world serpent. You will remember the story of the serpent as an enemy of God in the story of Adam and Eve, and the evil dragon in stories of heroes. The Romans brought the Wyvern in on their banners, and it became the symbol of Wessex and Wales. These are examples of how the old stories and symbols appear in different forms in various religions.

Friday is named after the goddess Frig, the goddess of love whose name probably meant 'darling'. In some stories she was the earth goddess, in some her daughter. She was worshipped in all lands from the crude Baalim of Canaan through Astarte, Aphrodite and the Roman Venus (vendredi). Her image is seen in most papers and magazines today! It has been argued that the worship of the earth-mother was older than that of the sky-father. The goddess had other names in Norse stories, but she was always the bearer of children and food for them. Her love for her son Balder is the best known story about her. The Roman writer Tacitus and the Saga of Olaf Tryggvason both describe the goddess being carried round on a covered cart, seen only by her husband. Tacitus described how her coming brought peace. After the tour, the cart and cover were washed in a pool and those who had seen inside to do so, were drowned. She was remembered in the stories of the Lady of the Lake in King Arthur. Sometimes images of the old gods were passed down by craftsmen and may be found in little stone and wood carvings in churches. There are over twenty 'sheelas' in England and many more in Ireland. These are crude female figures with big breasts like those found in all primitive religions. The Christian church developed the cult of the Virgin, the Mother of God, to rival the old religion. Sometimes they were able to continue the processions at the same time. Our present Mother's Day is close to the Feast of the Annunciation and the spring equinox.

The best-known image from the old religions is the Green Man. His face, like the Greek god Bacchus, has leaves in its mouth. He is to be seen in churches throughout Europe. His name is preserved in Jack-of-the-Green, at the Helston May dances and in the stories of Puck. He is probably the origin of Robin Hood as well. He is obviously connected with spring and new growth. He might be part of a story like that of Balder the god who has to die and, in the eastern forms, to rise again each spring. He was certainly the green knight killed by Sir Gawain.

We can only guess at what the Saxons believed and did from small clues. When schoolchildren today dance round a maypole their feelings are very different from Red Indians worshipping a totem pole, but that is what they are acting out. The pole itself may be connected with the Yggdrasill, the norse earth tree. They saw it as a great ash; we know of it in the Garden of Eden story. When they listened to the Christian preachers they probably heard a story about a tree, the cross. Celtic and Saxon crosses appear in all sorts of odd places. They heard about a dying god and his mother — and they used their own pictures in poetry and art as Christians. Bishop Daniel of Winchester wrote to tell Boniface how to preach to pagans. He was to let them claim parents for their gods, and then ask what came before and who ruled the universe first. He should ask why no more gods were being born.

'What again do the heathen mean to confer by their sacrifices upon the gods, who have all things under their sway; or why do the gods leave it in the power of those subject to them to decide what tribute to offer?'

So by gentle argument Boniface and his fellow preachers changed the ways of the German tribes. We find traditional Christian language about the blood of Jesus crude. To the Saxons, this was instead of the blood of their children. The missionaries built churches on the same

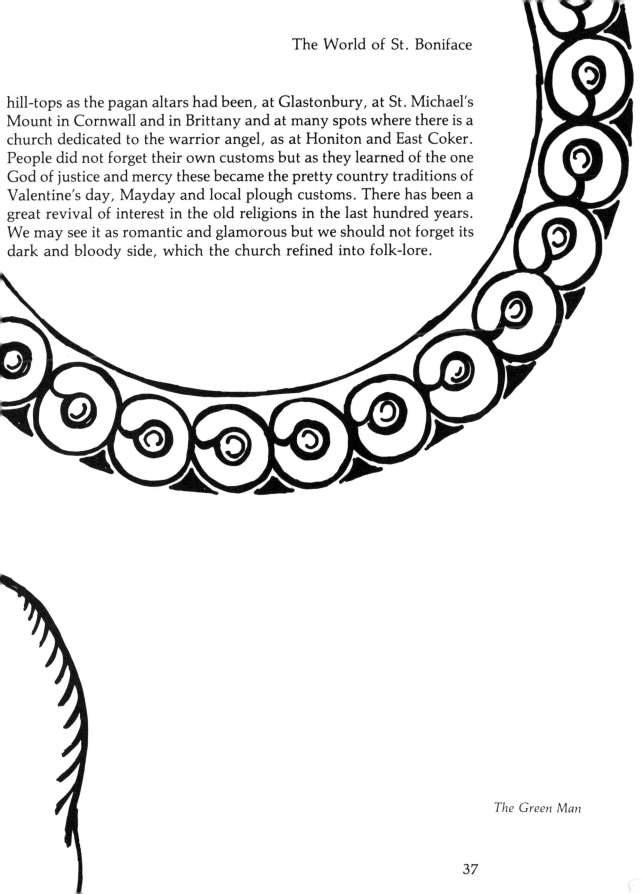

hill-tops as the pagan altars had been, at Glastonbury, at St. Michael's Mount in Cornwall and in Brittany and at many spots where there is a church dedicated to the warrior angel, as at Honiton and East Coker. People did not forget their own customs but as they learned of the one God of justice and mercy these became the pretty country traditions of Valentine's day, Mayday and local plough customs. There has been a great revival of interest in the old religions in the last hundred years. We may see it as romantic and glamorous but we should not forget its dark and bloody side, which the church refined into folk-lore.

The Green Man

chapter 3

the church of st Boniface

When we talk about the Roman Catholic church today we think of a great world-wide organisation with a leader whose election dominates world news. Since the sixteenth century western Europe has been divided into those who serve and those who fear the Pope. Now that we see the world divided into Christian and Moslem or Christian and atheist we are in a better position to understand the problems of the church in the time of St. Boniface. When he began his work, the united Catholic Europe which resisted the Turkish advance did not yet exist. The greatest power in Europe was still the Emperor at Constantinople. He became steadily weaker until the Turks captured the city in 1452.

All the Christians in western Europe had been converted from Rome, but in two distinct stages. The first churches had been founded under the Roman Empire by saints like Patrick in Ireland and Alban in England. The Celts remained Christian when the Saxon tribes invaded, but lost touch with the church in Rome. They sent preachers to their fellow Britons in Wales, Scotland and on the continent. They also preached to the invaders and left isolated churches behind them, usually in the course of pilgrimages to Rome. The second wave of missionaries were those sent from Rome like Augustine of Canterbury and his followers. In the more settled states of Europe they were able to keep in touch with Rome and with their own bishops. In the two hundred year interval when contact with Rome was lost, changes were made in the calendar and in ritual and discipline. Bede described the bitterness between the British bishops and Augustine when they met at Aust on the River Severn. The only way that rival forms of Christianity could be brought together was through the care of the Pope.

The Pope

The word 'pope' is the Latin word 'papa' and simply means father. It was used of the chief bishops of the church whose correct title was patriarch. In Russia it came to be used for every parish priest. The patriarchs of the early church were at Jerusalem, Alexandria, Antioch, Constantinople and Rome. After the Arab conquest, only two remained. In the east the Patriach was the servant of the emperor. In the west he made the conquering Goths Christians and the surviving churchmen preserved a little of Roman order in Gaul. The emperor won back part of Italy and ruled from Ravenna until 751, but after that the Pope had to turn to Pepin and then his son Charlemagne.

The claim to be head of the church in the west had first been made by Leo the Great who was Pope 440 - 461. His work was built on by Gregory the Great, Pope 590 - 604. He made peace with the Lombards without consulting the emperor and refused to recognise the patriarch of Constantinople as his lord. At some time during the next hundred and fifty years someone in Rome forged a will from the Emperor Constantine giving Italy to the Bishop of Rome. This was based upon a well-known legend about Pope Sylvester healing the emperor. In 754 Pepin made a similar gift to the Pope at his villa at Quiercy. He then went on to defeat Aistulf the King of the Lombards and to establish the Pope's rule in Italy. On Christmas Day 800 the Pope anointed Pepin's son Charles as the Holy Roman Emperor. This was a first attempt to unite the religious and military power in Europe.

There were gaps in the line, but writers in the middle ages looked back to this period as the foundation of chivalry. Their romances were wrong. Not all Frankish knights served God and protected the weak. They did inspire orders such as the Knights of the Temple and of St. John of Jerusalem who took vows like monks and defended the holy places. From the treaty between the Franks and the Pope which the work of Boniface had made possible there grew the pattern of feudalism in which every man and every priest had his lord, and in which a great pyramid of promises led to the Pope as the servant of the servants of God. This ideal pattern did not prevent wars, but at least it kept contact between Christian peoples which the reformation smashed. It failed to include the Eastern Church, though, and after conflicts over the conversion of the Slavs, the Patriarch and the Pope excommunicated each other in 1054.

The Archbishop

The patriarchs had been rulers of the church in quite small areas.

The Pope of Rome had been head of the church in Italy. When the empire became Christian, he had to care for the tribes in Gaul and Britain as well. When it fell, he found the converted Saxons in his care. Gregory I had sent Augustine to organise an English church. He had planned a centre at York the old Roman capital. The Anglo-Saxon church continued to depend on Rome. St. Wilfrid won the debate on the date of Easter by appealing to the authority of St. Peter. After thiis synod at Whitby in 664, St. Chad claimed to be Bishop of York. In 666 Wilfrid went to Rome for help. He went again in 678 and 704. He became archbishop of the north when Theodore of Tarsus, the Greek Archbishop of Canterbury, planned the church of England at the synods of Hertford in 673 and Hatfield in 680.

Theodore's reforms established the role of the archbishop as a metropolitan, that is ruler of the cities around him. One of Wilfrid's quarrels was about the division of York into four. The archbishop was responsible to the pope. His symbol came to be the pallium. This is a circular scarf with two bands decorated with six crosses. It looks like a Y when it is worn. Augustine received one as a gift, then Willibrord and Boniface as marks of special honour. In 744 Boniface had it sent to archbishop Grimo of Rouen. By the ninth century it became the essential badge of office for an archbishop, granted in return for the promise to obey the Pope.

The French church was never as closely tied to Rome as the English, which is one important reason why there was no reformation in France. Pepin refused to submit the Frankish church to the pattern laid down by the Pope. Charlemagne brought it into the system, but he was clearly the protector of the Pope and his lands. When Boniface began his work there were two kinds of church in Europe: the missionary churches of England and Frisia supported by the Pope; and the older churches which were more independent. Boniface's work as representative of the Pope and later as Archbishop of Mainz helped to make a common system with the Pope at its head.

The symbol of the pallium and the establishment of the college of cardinals established the authority of Rome over the whole of western and northern Europe. In the late fifteenth century America, Africa and Asia were added, but the system by then had become too big to survive. Long before the reformation, archbishops like Anselm, Thomas Becket and Stephen Langton were finding their loyalties divided between king and pope.

The Bishop

The Anglo-Saxon word 'biscop' was an attempt to say the Greek 'episcopos' which means overseer. It was another title in the New Testament for the elders of the churches. In the second century the church leaders divided into three ranks; the bishop, the presbyter, or priest, and the deacon. The apostles had laid hands on all those they left behind. This developed into three rites in the church: the consecration of bishops, the ordination of priests and making of deacons. Many churches have bishops, priests and deacons today, but they do not all mean the same thing by them.

In the early church the bishop was the head of the church in a city. That might have been a community of twenty families. He would be chairman at the Lord's table. Eventually his 'chair,' in Greek *kathedra*, became the name of a great and beautiful church, but it could just as well be in a wooden hut or a lock-up office. Another word used is the bishop's 'see' or seat, which has come to mean the same as diocese. This comes from the Greek for 'housekeeping'. As the churches grew larger, the bishop's work became more important. When rich officials like St. Ambrose were converted, the church made them bishops and after the conversion of Constantine in 323, the bishops became officials of the Empire. Constantine called them all to the council at his palace at Nicaea in 325 to agree on a creed. The emperors called a series of 'world' or general councils to decide problems of belief.

In western Europe there were very few bishops compared with Italy as there were few cities. Contact with Rome had broken down, and it became the custom for bishops to make new bishops, as Willibrord wished to do to Boniface. If a travelling saint had left a church to itself, the people would make their own bishop. If there was a quarrel in a city; rival bishops might appear. There were also bishops who did not accept the decisions of councils and who wandered from place to place. Boniface saw the effect of the synods in England and realised the value of a united and well-ordered church. We should realise that it was a thousand years before a country, the United States, was willing to allow total religious freedom. Before then catholics and protestants both thought that religion was very important in keeping people together. When Boniface was made a bishop the Pope gave him a book of church laws to follow. The Pope wanted to see one law in all the churches as a means of keeping peace. It was the duty of the bishop to protect his church. Trouble arose later when kings used

An artist's reconstruction of a Frankish monastery

bishops to do their work for them.

The Monastery

The word *monk* means someone who wants to be alone and *hermi* means someone who lives in a desert. All religions had men like this. Sometimes they lived alone in caves, some Christians in Egypt lived on the top of stone columns. Sometimes they lived in groups. In the Celtic church each monk would have a little hut in a compound and look after himself in this 'cell'. We can see the ruins of a Celtic monastery at Tintagel in Cornwall. Earlier cells were made of wood and were little more than tents. They found it necessary to join together for services and to discuss their work, so gradually a timetable grew up. St. Lawrence Chapel, Crediton, was once a hermitage.

The Welsh monk St. Columbanus founded the Abbey of Luxeuil in the sixth century. His followers built others in the lands ruled by the Franks, including the famous St. Gallen. These all followed his very strict rule. About 550 St. Benedict founded Monte Cassino in Italy and wrote for his monks the rule book which was to become used almost everywhere. It seems very strict to us: the monks were to keep an eye on each other all the time and never to waste any time, but it was easier than the rule of Columbanus. Boniface had learned the rule at Exeter and Nursling. All the monasteries he built followed the rule.

It was quite common for rich men to send their children to become monks. Kings like Carloman, Childeric and Ethelred of Mercia were sometimes glad to retire to monasteries and their widows were often sent to them. The rich brought generous gifts, and because they were used to ruling, they often became abbots or abbesses. The nunnery provided a home for unmarried daughters and unprotected sons. In England there was a tradition of having the two communities on the same site. Whitby was like this, and so was the only English order founded by St. Gilbert of Sempringham in the twelfth century.

The early monasteries were not all big. Sometimes there was just a small chapel and a house for two or three priests or monks. These were the minsters set up in missionary areas, like Ilminster, Axminster and Exminster. These sometimes became cathedrals, like York. They were served by a college, or collection of priests. If there was an abbey, these would be monks. If not, they would be canons under a similar rule. This organisation was used for controlling tutors and students at Oxford and Cambridge, and for the earliest grammar

The Church of St. Boniface, Nursling. The present building is fourteenth century

schools like Winchester College. It has survived the reformation in a few parish churches like Crediton and Ottery St. Mary. A college was stricter than a school because it controlled the whole day of fellows and students. The word has changed in meaning in the last twenty years.

Some places grew into the great abbeys which we know from the late middle ages. We may see them in ruins as at Tintern and Glastonbury or rebuilt as at Buckfast. This is a living testimony of what can be achieved by the gifts of the faithful combined with the labour of a few devoted men. Boniface had the first stone church built at Fulda. In times of peace when stone was plentiful and labour cheap, similar halls were built for the monks to read, eat, sleep and wash in. Benedict insisted that these should be done together. We still use the Latin words library, refectory, dormitory and lavatory. These were joined by a cloister to protect them from bad weather. (This is a function which does not seem to occur to the designers of modern schools and colleges!) Some monasteries took more than five hundred years to reach their final form. The monks were building for eternity.

Others have disappeared. Some were destroyed by the Vikings, some carted away by protestants. Bede's Wearmouth has disappeared. So has Boniface's Nursling, burnt in 800. There is a little archaeological evidence of an earthwork and causeway there. The monks may well have settled within the Roman walls as they did at Exeter, but we know of its existence only from the lives of the saint.

The King

If we want to see what early kings were like we can watch stags fighting to be leader of a herd of deer, or read about gang warfare. The strongest ruled a tribe, until someone was strong enough to defy him. As in the story of David and Saul, this might be a son or a general. The Greeks and Romans did not like kings. The Greek name was tyrant, the Roman dictator. Warlike tribes could not manage without one. The kings would claim to be descended from a god to add authority to their rule and to help pass it to their sons. The sons were often not as tough as their fathers and found strong men to rule for them. The Merovingian kings of the Franks had a 'majordomo', or mayor of the palace. These were the effective rulers. Pepin was the first in 687. He was followed by his son, Charles Martel, who saved France from the Moors in 732. This battle at Tours is one of the most

important in history. Boniface crowned his son king of the Franks in
752 and his son Charles received the greater title of Emperor in 800.

The anointing of Pepin first by Boniface and then by the Pope was
almost the first use of this ceremony in the west. It restored to the king
the claim he used to be able to make as the son of a god and made him
holy in the sight of his people so no-one would harm him. James I and
VI, the protestant King of England and Scotland, claimed to be able to
heal people by touching them. Boniface helped to start this idea of the
divine right of kings. This was to lead to quarrels with the Pope later.
In the east there was no question: the emperor appointed the
patriarch. In the west, the Pope claimed to appoint the king through
his archbishop, and to be able to remove him. The Pope was to
succeed with William Rufus and John in England, but failed with
Henry VIII. The king was not free to do as he liked. He had a duty to
God to protect his people and preserve true religion. This pattern
often did not work, but it was an ideal which helped Europe to recover
from the dark ages and progress towards civilisation again. Not until
1688 in England and 1789 in France is it possible to separate religion
and politics in history.

*St. Boniface's Well,
Crediton*

chapter 4

in the steps of st Boniface

Many readers will be attending special celebrations for the thirteenth hundredth anniversary of the birth of St. Boniface. Europe today looks very different from the seventh century, but churches still stand where the saint knew them and founded them. Devoted pilgrims or tourists would need to travel from Crediton to Nursling, Winchester, Canterbury and London where there are faint traces of Offa's time. They would need to travel 120 km up the Rhine to Wijk-bij-Duurstede, the Roman Batavodurum and visit Utrecht. They would want to go to north Friesland to see the site of the martyrdom at Dokkum. If they had a boat, they might put in at the tiny port of St. Josse-sur-Mer near Le Touquet, the medieval Cuentewick. From Picardy they would need to visit Soissons on the river Aisne 96 km from Paris where Pepin had his capital. They would then need to return to the Rhine to see Mainz and then across to the east of the Federal republic to see the great basilica at Fulda. If time allowed they should visit all Boniface's cathedrals in Hesse, Thuringia and Bavaria, and of course Rome itself. Boniface did not know the present St. Peter's and Vatican. He would have seen the Forum and the Colosseum and was probably received by the popes at the Lateran Palace.

Such a tour would be beyond the pocket and energy of most of us. Furthermore it could prove fruitless. To share the experience of the saint we would need to walk an unmade ridge road for day after day, pause and look at empty landscapes. We would need to kneel on the stone or mud floor of a church and join in the ancient prayers of the church. We would need the absolute conviction that God had revealed the correct way of life for men through the scriptures and through the rules of the church, and we would be prepared to apply these standards whatever the wishes of the powerful or the majority. In his day Boniface, like all great leaders of religion, was a non-conformist. His mission was to establish the rule of the church, which was a part of the preparation for the kingdom of God.

Part of our attempt to understand the traditions which have made modern Europe involves looking at the sites and buildings of the past. To benefit from this, the visitor needs knowledge as well as curiosity. This booklet has been written to give background information for the tourist as well as for the student. There is a good deal to see of the Exeter where Boniface studied and something of the Crediton where he was born.

The visitor to Devon should first visit one of the iron-age hill forts like Blackbury Castle near Colyton; Cadbury on the road from Crediton to Tiverton; or Posbury, the possible site of the battle of 661. In these quiet wooded places, neglected by the Romans and the Saxons, it is possible to imagine the empty tree-covered countryside of the seventh century with the smoke of a few settlements in the river valleys below. It is less easy to imagine them in time of danger, crowded with armed men with their families in rough wooden shelters and their cattle. There must have been water storage, possibly dew ponds. We have no idea what sort of resistance the Dunmonii put up to the west Saxons. These forts were ancient then. The first Elizabethans used some of them for beacons, we use them for television masts.

Crediton lies on high ground above the River Creedy. It is difficult to imagine any sort of boat navigating this now, but it was certainly the line of advance from the Exe Valley. The traditional birthplace of Winfrith and the site of the monastery is near Mill Street (1). This was founded by King Aethelhard of Wessex in 739 and witnessed by Boniface's friend Bishop Daniel and his pupil abbot Dud. The charter is the oldest and strongest evidence for the birth of the saint in the town. Few traces of the 'college' dissolved by Henry VIII remain. The magnificent parish church of the Holy Cross (2) is the successor to the lost St. Mary's Minster. The east window commemorates the 1897 jubilee and shows episodes in the life of the saint. A statue of Wynfrith —'St. Boniface-to-be' — by the Polish sculptor Witold Kawalec stands in the church and commemorates the 1980 celebrations. In the park (3) there is the ancient well of St. Boniface and the modern statue by Alan Durst was unveiled by Princess Margaret in 1960. The Roman Catholic parish church (4) was built in 1969. Its associations with its patron saint include a foundation stone from the Abbot of Fulda and a reredos of the felling of the oak at Geismar by Kenneth Carter.

Exeter has suffered from both bombing and rebuilding, but the lat-

est phase of redevelopment has revealed the medieval bridge and the church of St. Edmund, which was rebuilt in 1834. (8) It has also opened up stretches of the city walls and the energetic visitor should park in a long-stay car park and walk around the old city. This itinerary starts at the site of the Eastgate near the coach station and ends at the cathedral. The castle (1) was fortified by the Saxons and gave them control of the city and area around. From the Northernhay gardens (2) it is possible to appreciate the height of the city hill above the valley. The Rougemont Museum (3) has displays showing the early history of settlement in Devon. Cross the gardens and Queen

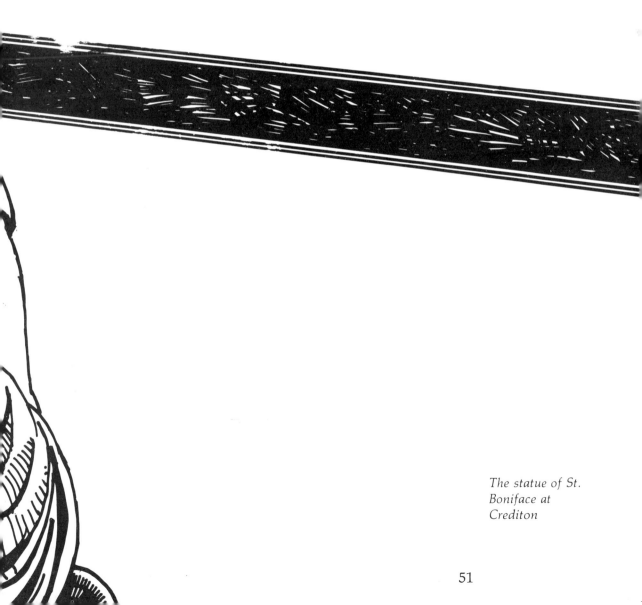

The statue of St. Boniface at Crediton

51

ƿ̄ lapa laurer ed Flaviani̇̄ Epu̇m
cons̄tantii̇̄ rðpatiẽlaın

INCIPIT EPISTVLᴀ
Dᴀ ꬱᴄ Lɮ̄   ᴀᴛ
RECꬱᴀᴏꬱꬱꬱDFLuıı
ᴀL ꞇ ꬱDı copum
ᴀꬱꬱULF·

caruifuo dmᴵ ıı   ı ıı ᴛ̄

*The Ragyndrudis
Codex at Fulda was
written about 700
AD and may have
been the book used
by the saint to
protect his head
(see p.20)*

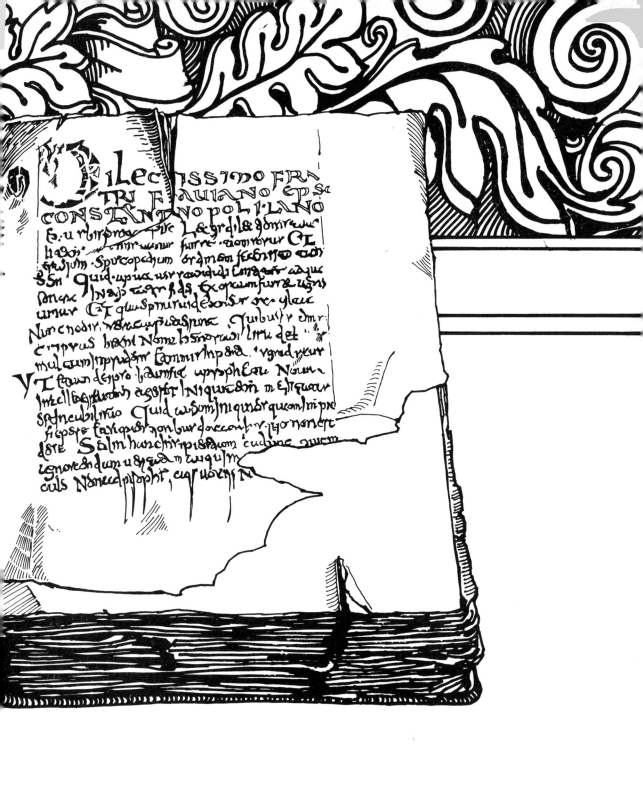

The Tomb of St. Boniface at Fulda

Street and visit St. Pancras Church (4) preserved in the heart of the Guildhall shopping precinct. Look at St. Mary Arches Church (5) then go away from the centre and walk along Bartholomew Street. In the Mint is St. Nicholas Priory, the only surviving monastic building (6). Cross Fore Street and descend to St. Mary Steps Church (7) which has part of the old Westgate in its structure. From here go down to the old bridge (8). The visitor with plenty of time and energy will wish to visit the quay and Maritime Museum. Otherwise, cut across the inner by-

pass, a dull steep walk, to South Street and the Cathedral Close (9).
This is one of the finest settings and buildings in Europe. There is no
trace of the Saxon buildings. St. Boniface is shown on the memorial
pulpit to another missionary martyr, Bishop Patteson. From the
Close, walk past the ruins of St. Catherine's Chapel (10) and the
underground passages (11). These are probably medieval rather than
Roman. There is a modern relief of the Saxon martyr St. Sidwell on a
shop front (12), near the church dedicated to her.

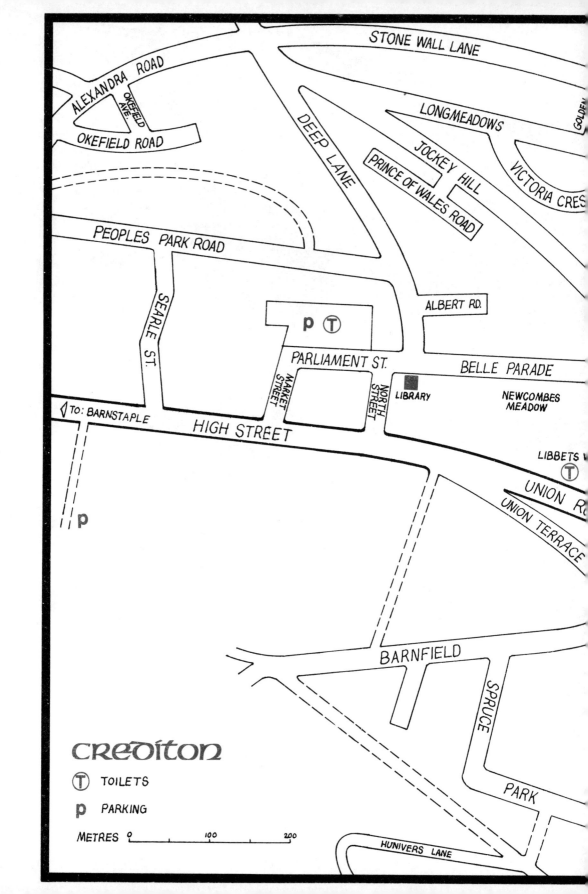

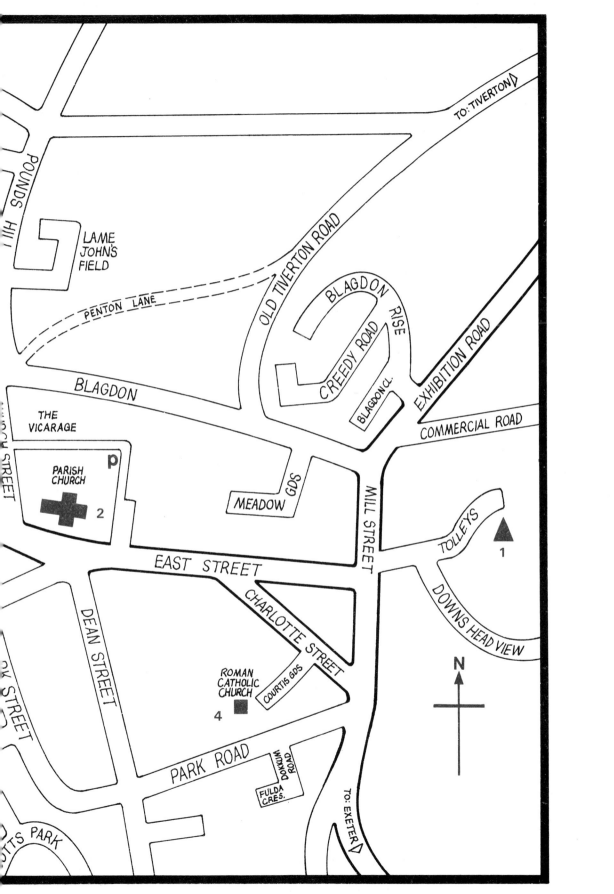

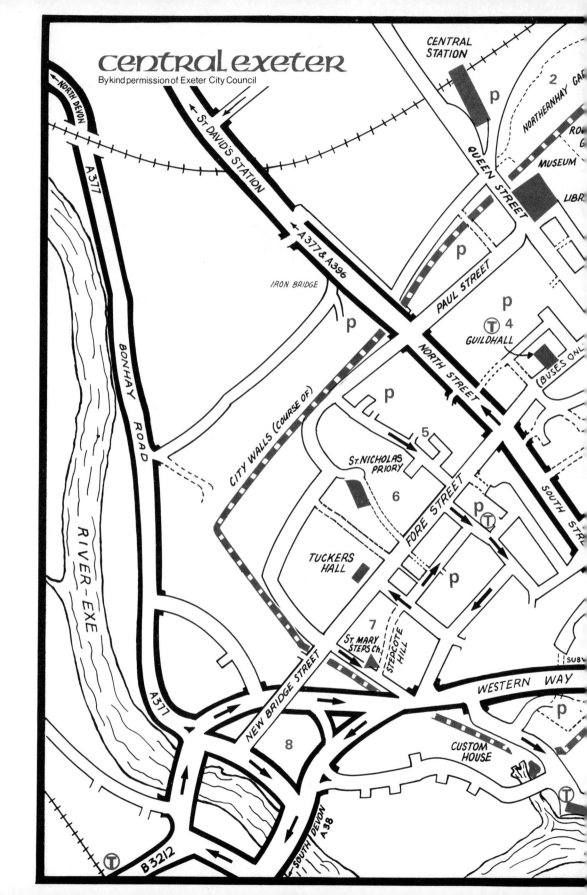

central exeter
By kind permission of Exeter City Council

CENTRAL STATION

2

NORTHERNHAY GARDENS

ROYAL GARDEN

MUSEUM

LIBRARY

QUEEN STREET

NORTH DEVON

A 377

St DAVID'S STATION

← A 377 & A396

IRON BRIDGE

PAUL STREET

p

p

p

4
GUILDHALL

(BUSES ONLY)

NORTH STREET

p

CITY WALLS (COURSE OF)

5

St. NICHOLAS PRIORY

6

FORE STREET

p

SOUTH STREET

BONHAY ROAD

RIVER-EXE

TUCKERS HALL

7
St MARY STEPS Ch.

STEPCOTE HILL

A 377

NEW BRIDGE STREET

8

SOUTH DEVON A 38

WESTERN WAY

CUSTOM HOUSE

p

SUBWAY

B 3212

CASTLE &
CROWN
COURT 1

UNIVERSITY OF EXETER

NORTH DEVON B3183

p

T

12

SIDWELL STREET

p

R.A.C.

SUMMERLAND STREET

CHEEKE STREET

B 3212

BUS & COACH
STATION

p

B 3183

SIDMOUTH

(BUSES ONLY)

UNDERGROUND
PASSAGES

11

PARIS STREET

CIVIC CENTRE
and T.I.C.

SWIMMING
BATH

HIGH STREET

T

PRINCESSHAY

p

p

P.O.

St. CATHERINE'S
CHAPEL

10

BEDFORD STREET

A.A.

SOUTHERNHAY WEST

p

Cathedral Close

BARNFIELD ROAD

WESTERN WAY

ST. PETER'S
CATHEDRAL

SOUTHERNHAY EAST

BARNFIELD
THEATRE

CLIFTON COURT

p

T

p

MAGDALEN ROAD

p

N

p

HOLLOWAY STREET B3182

MARITIME
MUSEUM

QUAY

EXMOUTH

RADFORD ROAD

PEDESTRIANS ONLY

T TOILETS

p PARKING

METRES 0   100   200

fuRtheR ReaDing

The Paternoster Press are publishing two important new books in 1980 to commemorate the work of Boniface:

Boniface of Devon, a biography by John Sladden, and
"The Greatest Englishman": Essays on St. Boniface and the Church at Crediton, ed. T. Reuter.

The most important source for the life and work of Boniface and his companions is their correspondence. One hundred and fifty letters have survived. These give a remarkable insight into the life of the times. Some of them are official letters and papers from the popes encouraging and confirming the work of the bishop. Others are personal to English friends, mostly monks and nuns. These show the warmth of the Saint's affection and give an idea of his charisma. In one he rebukes the King of Mercia for unchastity.

The latest edition of the complete correspondence was edited by M. Tangl in 1916. There are three volumes of selections in English:

1. Edward Kylie **The English Correspondence of St. Boniface** (*London 1911 and New York 1966*) contains letters 5, 9-11, 13-15, 23, 27, 29-36, 38, 46-7, 63-7, 69-76, 78-9, 81, 91, 94, 96-101, 103, 105, 111-2.
2. Ephraim Emerton **The Letters of St. Boniface** (*New York 1940*) contains letters 9-10, 12-30, 32-8, 40-52, 54, 56-65, 69-9, 72-91, 93-7,

99, 101, 103-9, 111, 115.

3. C. H. Talbot **The Anglo-Saxon Missionaries in Germany** *(London 1954)* contains letters 9, 11-12, 15-20, 22-30, 33-5, 40-1, 45-6, 48, 50-1, 59, 63, 68, 73, 75-6, 78, 91, 93, 95-6, 99, 101, 105, 107-9, 112. It also contains **Lives of Willibrord, Boniface, Willibald, Sturm, Leoba and Lebuin.**
G. F. Brown **Boniface of Crediton and his Companions** *(London 1910)* is detailed and discursive. Wilhelm Levison **England and the Continent in the Eighth Century** *(Oxford 1946)* puts the work of the Saint into context. There is renewed interest in the pre-Christian relations of Europe. Brian Branston **The Lost gods of England** *(London 1957)* and John Sharkey **Celtic Mysteries** *(London 1975)* are useful illustrated surveys. The case for the early Saxon settlement of Devon was made by W. G. Hoskins in **The Westward Expansion of Wessex** *(Leicester 1960).*

The anniversary of the martyrdom was marked by George William Greenaway **Saint Boniface. Three biographical studies for the Twelfth Centenary Festival** *(London 1955).*

There are several translations of Bede and the Anglo-Saxon Chronicle. I have quoted from **The Anglo-Saxon Chronicle** edited by Dorothy Whitelock, *(London 1961).*

the life and times

Events in the Life of Boniface		Events in Europe
	658	Cenwealh beat the Britons at Peonnan
	661	Cenwealh beat the Britons at Posenbrig
	664	Synod of Whitby
Born at Crediton	680	
	682	Centwine defeated the Britons
Entered the monastery at Exeter	685 -87	Pepin II united Franks
	692	St. Willibrord to Utrecht
Monk at Nursling	700	
Ordained priest	710	
? Mission to Canterbury	715	Gregory II Pope 715 - 31
Visit to Frisia	716 -41	Charles Martel ruled Franks
ROME: Mission to Bavaria, Thuringia, Frisia and Hesse	718 -19	
ROME: Bishop to Hesse and Thuringia: Thor's oak	722 -23	
	731	Gregory III Pope 731-41
Archbishop Boniface	732	Battle or Tours (or Poitiers)

# of st Boniface

Events in the Life of Boniface		Events in Europe
	735	Death of Bede
ROME: Reform of Bavaria	738	Death of Willibrord:
	-39	monastery at Crediton
Reform of Hesse and Thuringia	741	Zacharias Pope 741-52 Pepin III and Carloman
First Council of East Frankish Church	742	
Second Council of East Franks	743	Birth of Charlemagne
Council of West Franks (Soissons): Fulda founded	744	
Council of whole Frankish Church	745	Synod of Rome confirmed Soissons
Archbishop of Mainz	746	
Carloman became a monk	747	
	751	Fall of Exarchate of Ravenna
Coronation of Pepin	752	Stephen II, Pope 752-7
Resignation of Boniface	754	'Donation of Quiercy'
Martyred at Dokkum	755	
	768	Charlemagne King of the Franks
	800	Holy Roman Emperor
	814	Death of Charlemagne

A PRAYER

Almighty God,
who gave grace to your servant Boniface
to bring light and order to the
peoples of Europe,
Give us grace
that we may seek to live as one people
with those of different tongues,
that we may make homes
where your way is followed,
that we may seek truth, understanding
and love
throughout our lives,
Through Jesus Christ our Lord,
Amen